I0045949

Join the growing global Radio Entrepreneurs community as we share the many dynamic stories of entrepreneurship and chronicle the myriad issues faced by entrepreneurs today.

Visit our website at http://radioentrepreneurs.com or get in touch with us through Google Plus, Twitter (@BizOnTheRadio), and Facebook.

Jeffrey S. Davis and Mark Cohen
on The 24-Hour Turnaround

How Amazing Entrepreneurs Succeed In Tough Times

# Jeffrey S. Davis and Mark Cohen

## THiNKaha®

## An Actionable Business Journal

E-mail: info@thinkaha.com
20660 Stevens Creek Blvd., Suite 210
Cupertino, CA 95014

Copyright © 2017, Jeffrey S. Davis  and Mark Cohen

All rights reserved. No part of this book shall be reproduced, stored in a retrieval system, or transmitted by any means other than through the AHAthat platform or with the same attribution shown in AHAthat without written permission from the publisher.

⇨ Please go to http://aha.pub/24turnaround to read this AHAbook and to share the individual AHAmessages that resonate with you.

Published by THiNKaha®
20660 Stevens Creek Blvd., Suite 210, Cupertino, CA 95014
http://thinkaha.com
E-mail: info@thinkaha.com

First Printing: May 2017
Hardcover  ISBN: 978-1-61699-206-4 1-61699-206-9
Paperback ISBN: 978-1-61699-207-1 1-61699-207-7
eBook ISBN: 978-1-61699-208-8 1-61699-208-5
Place of Publication: Silicon Valley, California, USA
Paperback Library of Congress Number: 2017932240

**Trademarks**

All terms mentioned in this book that are known to be trademarks or service marks have been appropriately capitalized. Neither THiNKaha, nor any of its imprints, can attest to the accuracy of this information. Use of a term in this book should not be regarded as affecting the validity of any trademark or service mark.

**Warning and Disclaimer**

Every effort has been made to make this book as complete and as accurate as possible. The information provided is on an "as is" basis. The author(s), publisher, and their agents assume no responsibility for errors or omissions. Nor do they assume liability or responsibility to any person or entity with respect to any loss or damages arising from the use of information contained herein.

## Dedication

The inspiration for all good things comes from those closest to us.

With love,

Michael, Rachel, and Sandy

Stephanie, Joshua, and Wendy

# Acknowledgments

Special thanks to Wendy and Sandy. Your help with the book was invaluable. We could not have done this without you.

# How to Read a THiNKaha® Book
## A Note from the Publisher

The THiNKaha series is the CliffsNotes of the 21st century. The value of these books is that they are contextual in nature. Although the actual words won't change, their meaning will change every time you read one as your context will change. Experience your own "AHA!" moments ("AHAmessages™") with a THiNKaha book; AHAmessages are looked at as "actionable" moments—think of a specific project you're working on, an event, a sales deal, a personal issue, etc. and see how the AHAmessages in this book can inspire your own AHAmessages, something that you can specifically act on. Here's how to read one of these books and have it work for you:

1.  Read a THiNKaha book (these slim and handy books should only take about 15–20 minutes of your time!) and write down one to three actionable items you thought of while reading it. Each journal-style THiNKaha book is equipped with space for you to write down your notes and thoughts underneath each AHAmessage.

2.  Mark your calendar to re-read this book again in 30 days.

3.  Repeat step #1 and write down one to three more AHAmessages that grab you this time. I guarantee that they will be different than the first time. BTW: this is also a great time to reflect on the actions taken from the last set of AHAmessages you wrote down.

After reading a THiNKaha book, writing down your AHAmessages, re-reading it, and writing down more AHAmessages, you'll begin to see how these books contextually apply to you. THiNKaha books advocate for continuous, lifelong learning. They will help you transform your ahas into actionable items with tangible results until you no longer have to say "AHA!" to these moments—they'll become part of your daily practice as you continue to grow and learn.

As The AHA Guy at THiNKaha, I definitely practice what I preach. I read 2-3 AHAbooks a month in addition to those that we publish and take away two to three different action items from each of them every time. Please e-mail me your AHAs today!

Mitchell Levy
publisher@thinkaha.com

**THiNK**aha®

# Contents

# Section  I

## Introduction to the 24-Hour Principles

There is no clear-cut formula for achieving business success, but the ten "24-Hour Principles of Success" enclosed in this AHAbook will surely pave your way to an outstanding performance at work. So, what are you waiting for? Learn from these principles now and start making a big difference!

# 1

In 24 hours, make a quick and concrete change for your company. It can have a lasting effect. @BizOnTheRadio

_____

_____

_____

# 2

Who are entrepreneurs? They are the engine that fuels job growth in a country. http://radioentrepreneurs.com @BizOnTheRadio

_____

_____

_____

# 3

The leader you are today is the sum of everything that's happened to you up to this point. @BizOnTheRadio

_____

_____

_____

# 4

The ability to act and not just react fast is what "The 24-Hour Turnaround" is all about. Learn more from this book! @BizOnTheRadio

_____

_____

_____

# 5

Implement the "24-Hour Principles for Success" and start to see evidence of improvement within 24 hours. @BizOnTheRadio

_____

_____

_____

# 6

24-Hour Turnaround Principle 1 of 10:
Have a vision and strategic plan reflecting
a leader's personality, goals,
and industry. @BizOnTheRadio

_____

_____

_____

# 7

24-Hour Turnaround Principle 2 of 10:
Make a set of guiding principles and code
of conduct for employees
to follow. @BizOnTheRadio

_____

_____

_____

# 8

24-Hour Turnaround Principle 3 of 10: Communicate relentlessly with your employees. http://radioentrepreneurs.com @BizOnTheRadio

_____

_____

_____

# 9

24-Hour Turnaround Principle 4 of 10:
Create a strong financial plan for your
company. @BizOnTheRadio

_____

_____

_____

# 10

24-Hour Turnaround Principle 5 of 10:
Constantly raise the bar -- develop your
organization toward success
and leadership. @BizOnTheRadio

_____

_____

_____

# 11

24-Hour Turnaround Principle 6 of 10:
Get the team involved when making tough
decisions, but be the final
decision maker. @BizOnTheRadio

_____

_____

_____

# 12

24-Hour Turnaround Principle 7 of 10:
Accept help and support from talented,
trusted advisors. No one knows
everything. @BizOnTheRadio

_____

_____

_____

# 13

24-Hour Turnaround Principle 8 of 10:
Expect excellence from everyone -- train
and develop employees for professional
growth. @BizOnTheRadio

_____

_____

_____

# 14

24-Hour Turnaround Principle 9 of 10:
Implement and use technology to monitor,
manage, finance, and grow the
organization. @BizOnTheRadio

_____

_____

_____

# 15

24-Hour Turnaround Principle 10 of 10:
Facilitate continuous positive action.
Plan for the growth of your
organization. @BizOnTheRadio

_____

_____

_____

# 16

Do you have what it takes to be the leader of your organization? Apply the 24-Hour Turnaround Principles! @BizOnTheRadio

_____

_____

_____

# 17

"The 24-Hour Turnaround" is about the companies most of us operate or work for and have no option other than to succeed. @BizOnTheRadio

_____

_____

_____

# 18

Find your own voice, follow your dreams, and pursue the things you believe in. http://radioentrepreneurs.com @BizOnTheRadio

_____

_____

_____

# 19

Live your dream. Do not put boundaries around it. http://radioentrepreneurs.com @BizOnTheRadio

_____

_____

_____

# Section II

## Shared Expectations in a Business Relationship

Business relationships are indeed challenging and complex in nature. However, you are not alone in this journey! Business leaders, colleagues, clients, or even your family can assist you toward building a stronger and more profitable organization. Take a quick look at some of these shared expectations that can be formed in a business relationship!

# 20

Entrepreneurship is not for the faint of heart. Be an economic hero!
http://radioentrepreneurs.com
@BizOnTheRadio

_____

_____

_____

# 21

The challenge for a leader is to always handle unexpected difficult situations humanely but quickly. Are you up to it?
http://aha.pub/JerryHyman-LI

_____

_____

_____

# 22

High expectations start from the top.
Employees expect the leader to pull
them out from the mess you are in.
http://aha.pub/KarenBressler-LI

_____

_____

_____

# 23

Leading an enterprise involves personal
sacrifice, loneliness, and fear. Are you
prepared for it?
http://radioentrepreneurs.com
@BizOnTheRadio

_____

_____

_____

# 24

Economic heroes take risks in order
to achieve levels of success most
entrepreneurs only dream of.
http://radioentrepreneurs.com
@BizOnTheRadio

_____

_____

_____

# 25

A leader's job is to grow the business and to grow the people. Both are equally important. http://radioentrepreneurs.com http://aha.pub/KenFerry-LI

---

---

---

# 26

When a business grows, the challenge of jobs expands beyond the scope of the incumbent. Can you and your people handle it? @BizOnTheRadio

---

---

---

# 27

Retailers seem to be blaming the suppliers
if goods are not selling. Don't you think it's
such an insane economy?
http://aha.pub/JoelRabinowitz-LI

_____

_____

_____

# 28

A leader expects their employees to do their very best. If they do, they will reap good fruits of their labor. @BizOnTheRadio

_____

_____

_____

# 29

When you love your job and you love your family, you're between two loves. There will always be an issue.
http://aha.pub/RussellRobinson-LI

_____

_____

_____

# 30

Family-owned businesses are a challenge. The business will always reflect the family, for better or for worse. @BizOnTheRadio

_____

_____

_____

# 31

The work is never done because what needs to be accomplished is never finished -- there are always more projects. @JNFRobinson

_____

_____

_____

# 32

Life is a continuous learning process.
There is no prescribed method to learn things.
http://radioentrepreneurs.com
http://aha.pub/JerryHyman-LI

_____

_____

_____

# Section III

## Attitudes That Define a Business Leader

Are you eager to become successful in leading your business? If you are, then unravel these essential attitudes toward achieving your life-long dream! Do you already have these attitudes? Or do you still need to learn and obtain them?

# 33

Leaders lead change. Doing nothing or staying with the status quo is not an option.
http://radioentrepreneurs.com
@BizOnTheRadio

_____

_____

_____

# 34

A good business leader stays calm,
never yells, and doesn't lose their temper.
Are you one? http://radioentrepreneurs.com
http://aha.pub/JerryHyman-LI

_____

_____

_____

# 35

Never give up. Stay focused on your goals.
http://radioentrepreneurs.com
@BizOnTheRadio

_____

_____

_____

# 36

Be loyal -- take the unwritten agreement you have with your team very seriously!
http://radioentrepreneurs.com
@BizOnTheRadio

_____

_____

_____

# 37

Never lose sight of the goal. Be generous in rewarding the team that ensures your company reaches its lofty goals. @BizOnTheRadio

———————————————

———————————————

———————————————

# 38

Be respectful. Treat people the way you want to be treated. Just like karma, what goes around, comes around. http://aha.pub/JoelRabinowitz-LI

———————————————

———————————————

———————————————

# 39

Are you determined to be an innovator
in an industry allergic to innovation?
Say "Yes"! http://radioentrepreneurs.com
http://aha.pub/KarenBressler-LI

_____

_____

_____

# 40

Instead of being the smartest one,
read, disseminate information,
and encourage others to do well.
http://aha.pub/KarenBressler-LI

_____

_____

_____

# 41

When you get all mucked up in your thoughts, always step back and ask yourself: "What's best for my company?"
http://aha.pub/KarenBressler-LI

_____

_____

_____

# 42

No matter what crisis your organization may face, always be up to the challenge.
http://radioentrepreneurs.com
@BizOnTheRadio

_____

_____

_____

# 43

Stay true to your personality.
Have fun turning your dreams into reality!
http://radioentrepreneurs.com
http://aha.pub/JoelRabinowitz-LI

---

---

---

# 44

Appreciate "Thank you" messages from
your employees. It shows a lot of respect.
http://radioentrepreneurs.com
http://aha.pub/JerryHyman-LI

---

---

---

# 45

Ignore your demons and put your
personal baggage behind you. Can you?
http://radioentrepreneurs.com
http://aha.pub/RichardCohen-LI

_____

_____

_____

# 46

To be a catalyst for change, lead by example.
http://radioentrepreneurs.com
@BizOnTheRadio

---
---
---

# 47

Be the moral compass for your company.
Commit unwaveringly to personal and
professional integrity.
http://radioentrepreneurs.com
@BizOnTheRadio

---
---
---

# Section IV

## Tips for Growing a Successful Business

Many people think that it's easy to make money in business, but they find out that the real process of growing a business is way more difficult than they thought. Therefore, take time to read and make use of these simple yet practical guidelines for turning your business venture into a success!

# 48

Develop a vision and get people to believe in it. Have you?
http://radioentrepreneurs.com
@BizOnTheRadio

_____

_____

_____

# 49

Everybody can improve in leading a business, and perhaps through reading, you can actually elevate your abilities.
http://aha.pub/JerryHyman-LI

_____

_____

_____

# 50

Bring all employees together around a common set of goals.
http://radioentrepreneurs.com
@BizOnTheRadio

_____

_____

_____

# 51

Develop people from within -- use cross-training to move people within the company. http://aha.pub/JerryHyman-LI

_____

_____

_____

# 52

Employee development is a priority in building a business. Are you developing yours well? @BizOnTheRadio

_____

_____

_____

# 53

Psychology can be far more useful
in running a company -- read,
understand, and motivate people.
http://aha.pub/JerryHyman-LI

_____

_____

_____

# 54

Be a different kind of supplier. Spend
more time engaging with your customers.
http://radioentrepreneurs.com
http://aha.pub/KarenBressler-LI

_____

_____

_____

# 55

Do not hesitate to make complex and unpopular decisions for your company. Stand up and say, "Do it this way."
http://aha.pub/KarenBressler-LI

_____

_____

_____

# 56

If you don't have good professional advisors from day one, your business may not succeed. http://aha.pub/RichardCohen-LI

_____

_____

_____

# 57

No matter how interesting the work may be, learn when to say "no." Know your strengths.
http://radioentrepreneurs.com
http://aha.pub/RichardCohen-LI

_____

_____

_____

# 58

Don't outsource equipment for
your business. Re-invest and buy.
http://radioentrepreneurs.com
http://aha.pub/RichardCohen-LI

_____

_____

_____

# 59

Be positive, stay positive, and respect everybody who works around you.
http://aha.pub/RichardCohen-LI

_____

_____

_____

# 60

Find a balance between constantly working and being with the family.
http://radioentrepreneurs.com
http://aha.pub/RichardCohen-LI

_____

_____

_____

# 61

Nobody is perfect. In business, you do make mistakes. Be sorry and learn from it.
http://radioentrepreneurs.com
http://aha.pub/RichardCohen-LI

_____

_____

_____

# 62

Take chances! If you don't take chances now, you're not going to make it. Believe in yourself! http://aha.pub/RichardCohen-LI

_____

_____

_____

# 63

Work with a Board that will help you succeed.
http://radioentrepreneurs.com
@BizOnTheRadio

_____

_____

_____

# 64

Do you have any social connections?
They can be your business partners.
http://radioentrepreneurs.com
http://aha.pub/JoelRabinowitz-LI

_____

_____

_____

# 65

Do not let any setbacks slow you down.
Use it as a learning opportunity to open
and run a business.
http://radioentrepreneurs.com
@BizOnTheRadio

_____

_____

_____

# 66

Fixing technology could take years to improve it, but fixing sales and marketing is something you can do a lot faster. http://aha.pub/KenFerry-LI

_____

_____

_____

# 67

Celebrate the successes of your company. Even if it's a tough time, do it to recognize your people's efforts. @BizOnTheRadio

_____

_____

_____

# 68

Reward your people financially.
Personal success is a blend of people's
success and financial success.
http://aha.pub/KenFerry-LI

_____

_____

_____

# 69

Do you want to stay on top? Work for it to
continuously improve and achieve even
greater heights. @BizOnTheRadio

_____

_____

_____

# 70

Always have a long-range strategy --
it doesn't have to be written.
http://radioentrepreneurs.com
@BizOnTheRadio

_____

_____

_____

# 71

To build success, focus on values
and attract new staff with those values.
http://radioentrepreneurs.com
@BizOnTheRadio

_____

_____

_____

# 72

Dig into the details. Know the numbers
and indicators that can make or
break your business. @BizOnTheRadio

_____

_____

_____

# 73

Get the right people in place with the right skills and mindset.

http://radioentrepreneurs.com

@BizOnTheRadio

_____

_____

_____

# 74

Despite professional and personal pressures, a strategic vision for your company will help you make it through.
http://aha.pub/KarenBressler-LI

_____

_____

_____

# 75

You have to believe in what you're delivering and then deliver it as best you can. http://aha.pub/RussellRobinson-LI

_____

_____

_____

# 76

Management style is a reflection of business goals combined with personal values and experiences. @BizOnTheRadio

_____

_____

_____

# 77

If you don't take hiring very seriously, you'll regret it. It should be as serious as firing!
http://aha.pub/RussellRobinson-LI

_____

_____

_____

# 78

To be able to put your head down and focus on one big problem at a time, get the right people into the right positions! http://aha.pub/KarenBressler-LI

_____

_____

_____

# 79

Nothing happens unless you make it happen. Try to stir things up! http://aha.pub/KarenBressler-LI

_____

_____

_____

# 80

If your business is on a better footing,
never take it for granted. Work as if it
can all go back in the tank again!
http://aha.pub/KarenBressler-LI

---

---

---

# 81

Take risks that your competitors may not.
If it doesn't work out, dust yourselves
off and try something else.
@BizOnTheRadio

---

---

---

# 82

A good barometer to know how the company is performing is to get personally involved.
http://radioentrepreneurs.com
http://aha.pub/JerryHyman-LI

_____

_____

_____

# 83

If an employee is unable to grow as the company grew, let them go for their own good and for the good of the company.
http://aha.pub/JerryHyman-LI

_____

_____

_____

# 84

Business boils down to economics -- know the margins and stay a step ahead of everyone else. @BizOnTheRadio

_____

_____

_____

# 85

Getting finances in order is a
top priority. Watch it like a hawk!
http://radioentrepreneurs.com
http://aha.pub/RussellRobinson-LI

_____

_____

_____

# 86

Learn from adversity in your life and from the company's history.
http://radioentrepreneurs.com
@BizOnTheRadio

_____

_____

_____

# 87

The only way to fix things is by careful prioritization. Are you dealing yours appropriately? @BizOnTheRadio

_____

_____

_____

# 88

Tackle the mess -- fix things sequentially but play to your strengths.
http://radioentrepreneurs.com
@BizOnTheRadio

_____

_____

_____

# 89

Build on a solid vision and never stop believing.
http://radioentrepreneurs.com
@BizOnTheRadio

_____

_____

_____

# 90

Don't be just a doll that can be dusted
off the shelf to show to people.
Step out and take more responsibility!
http://aha.pub/KarenBressler-LI

_____

_____

_____

# 91

Does your staff embrace using technology to help the company function better?
They better be!
http://radioentrepreneurs.com
@BizOnTheRadio

_____

_____

_____

# 92

How knowledgeable are your employees at using technology? Measure their abilities and train them.
http://radioentrepreneurs.com
@BizOnTheRadio

_____

_____

_____

# 93

If you want to succeed in business, hire people who possess special character. Choose wisely!
http://aha.pub/RichardCohen-LI

_____

_____

_____

# 94

Don't compromise the company for anyone.
If an employee is toxic to the
organization, make them leave.
http://aha.pub/KarenBressler-LI

_____

_____

_____

# 95

In order to succeed in business,
you have to fear failing. Surprisingly,
fear can help. @BizOnTheRadio

_____

_____

_____

# Section V

## Strengthening Employee and Customer Relationships

Have you ever thought about the essence of your employees and customers? They are the core elements for the survival of your organization. Thus, solidify your relationships with them by using the following strategies.

# 96

Enjoy the benefit of being challenged.
Invite criticism and feedback.
What's your management style?
http://aha.pub/KarenBressler-LI

_____

_____

_____

# 97

If your team thinks your decision is wrong,
encourage them to tell you why.
Can they propose a better solution?
http://aha.pub/KarenBressler-LI

_____

_____

_____

# 98

To communicate effectively, listen and understand the other person's perspective. Explain the final decision and why.
http://aha.pub/KarenBressler-LI

---

---

---

# 99

A person's position in the company does not matter. Be empathetic to everyone.
http://radioentrepreneurs.com
http://aha.pub/KarenBressler-LI

---

---

---

# 100

To make things work, customer care
during the worst times is key. That's the
power of personal relationships.
http://aha.pub/KarenBressler-LI

_____

_____

_____

# 101

Great employees and customers are the company's survival on a day-to-day basis.
http://aha.pub/KarenBressler-LI

_____

_____

_____

# 102

A business relationship is like a love affair. It needs to be carefully nurtured in good and bad times.
http://aha.pub/RichardCohen-LI

_____

_____

_____

# 103

Leadership is about communication
and respect. Do you treat your
staff and customers well?
http://radioentrepreneurs.com
http://aha.pub/RichardCohen-LI

_____

_____

_____

# 104

If somebody has a personal issue in the office about their family, send them home. Family is more important than work. http://aha.pub/RichardCohen-LI

---

---

---

# 105

To work on issues openly and collaboratively, give and get honest feedback. http://radioentrepreneurs.com http://aha.pub/KarenBressler-LI

---

---

---

# 106

Empower others and demonstrate the
trust you have in them.
http://radioentrepreneurs.com
@BizOnTheRadio

_____

_____

_____

# 107

Set the right tone for your company. Don't
look worried, your staff will sense panic!
http://radioentrepreneurs.com
http://aha.pub/KarenBressler-LI

_____

_____

_____

# 108

Practice good communication. Ensure your employees are not afraid to tell you anything. http://radioentrepreneurs.com http://aha.pub/JerryHyman-LI

_____

_____

_____

# 109

Balance the needs of the company
with the needs of its employees.
Are you doing that? @BizOnTheRadio

---

# 110

Improve your work environment.
Tried introducing the theme of fun
at work? It could be exciting!
http://aha.pub/KarenBressler-LI

# 111

Meet new employees and know them by name. Can you do that?
http://radioentrepreneurs.com
@BizOnTheRadio

_____

_____

_____

# 112

Recognize employees for their contributions. Reward them!
http://radioentrepreneurs.com
@BizOnTheRadio

_____

_____

_____

# 113

Set goals and coach your employees to improve interpersonally. Classes are not the answer. http://radioentrepreneurs.com http://aha.pub/KenFerry-LI

_____

_____

_____

# Section VI

## Signs of Business Growth and Success

The potential for growth and expansion is among the reasons why people start up their own businesses. How do you know if your organization is effectively growing? Here are a few indicators to check for.

# 114

Not all employees will love you, but if your team achieves success, you will gain their respect to follow you.
http://aha.pub/KarenBressler-LI

_____

_____

_____

# 115

With success, employee morale increases.
http://aha.pub/KarenBressler-LI

_____

_____

_____

# 116

A sign of a company's growing health
is when capable people leave and it
isn't quite as traumatic as it used to be.
http://aha.pub/KarenBressler-LI

_____

_____

_____

# 117

Having a vision, a plan, and delivering on that plan equals success.
http://radioentrepreneurs.com
@BizOnTheRadio

_____

_____

_____

# 118

Failure is not an option. In order to succeed in business, be strategic.
http://radioentrepreneurs.com
http://aha.pub/KarenBressler-LI

_____

_____

_____

# 119

If the organization is not preparing to grow,
then the organization is definitely moving
in the wrong direction. @BizOnTheRadio

_____

_____

_____

# Section VII

## How to Survive in a Shifting, Uncertain Economy

The economic market has never been in a fixed
state; it is always fluctuating. Rather than wait
for the negative impact it may bring to your
business, take the necessary steps to survive
during turbulent times. After all, it's for the
sake of your organization.

# 120

When you are challenged, don't change your beliefs about how you want to run your business. @BizOnTheRadio

_____

_____

_____

# 121

In order to keep your organization moving forward, make good use of technology. http://aha.pub/RussellRobinson-LI

_____

_____

_____

# 122

If you want an economic recovery,
be a proactive and not a reactive
entrepreneur. @BizOnTheRadio

_____

_____

_____

# 123

At the start, bringing in people you know
is vital. But if you want your company
to survive, you can bring in new people.
http://aha.pub/KenFerry-LI

_____

_____

_____

# 124

Conventional wisdom is wrong.
Humble, nice, and thoughtful people
can survive in highly competitive industries.
@BizOnTheRadio

_____

_____

_____

# 125

You don't need to have all the money
in the world to make an impact.
But you have to use the money well.
http://aha.pub/RussellRobinson-LI

_____

_____

_____

# 126

If you didn't make mistakes,
you haven't tried anything. To make your
organization stronger, learn from it.
http://aha.pub/RussellRobinson-LI

_____

_____

_____

# 127

Wouldn't it be effective if you make your staff look at everything they're doing as if it's their own business? Try it.
http://aha.pub/RussellRobinson-LI

---
---
---

# 128

If employees do their jobs and they do them well, they become happy. If they don't, they don't work for me.
http://aha.pub/RichardCohen-LI

---
---
---

# 129

Empower employees to make decisions responsibly. Whether it's a good or bad decision, support them!
http://radioentrepreneurs.com
@BizOnTheRadio

_____

_____

_____

# 130

Your competition is only yourself. Chase your competition out of your business.
http://radioentrepreneurs.com
http://aha.pub/RussellRobinson-LI

_____

_____

_____

# 131

Building a business is understanding that it's a matter of what people want to buy, not what you're selling them.
http://aha.pub/RussellRobinson-LI

---

---

---

# 132

With consistent, concise, and clear communication, improved productivity at all levels results. @BizOnTheRadio

---

---

---

# 133

It's a fine balancing act -- perish tomorrow or provide the top service/product while whittling out the margin killers.
http://aha.pub/KarenBressler-LI

_____

_____

_____

# 134

Being an entrepreneur means never really dealing with survival. That makes entrepreneurship not that risky.
http://aha.pub/JoelRabinowitz-LI

_____

_____

_____

# 135

They teach you values and survival skills to shape your future. Get them from your parents.
http://aha.pub/JoelRabinowitz-LI

_____

_____

_____

# 136

The model for how we need to work is changing daily. Have you learned to adapt your plan? http://radioentrepreneurs.com http://aha.pub/JoelRabinowitz-LI

_____

_____

_____

# 137

The best organizations develop from within.
Are you one of the best?
http://radioentrepreneurs.com
@BizOnTheRadio

_____

_____

_____

# 138

For leaders to better diagnose themselves, their organizations, and their marketplace, use the 24-Hour Principles as a guide. @BizOnTheRadio

_____

_____

_____

# 139

To survive and thrive in the face of economic uncertainty, make the practical changes in 24 hours. @BizOnTheRadio

_____

_____

_____

# 140

Aspiring to be a 24-Hour Leader? Measure your own organization against the 24-Hour Turnaround Principles. @BizOnTheRadio

_____

_____

_____

# About the Authors

**Jeffrey S. Davis** is CEO and founder of Mage LLC, one of New England's leading strategic organizational management and family consulting firms. Jeffrey is Chairman of the Board for both MTP Software, a leader in the sports CRM category, and The Social Scene, a breakthrough social app. Jeffrey is founder and hosts the daily internet business radio show, "Radio Entrepreneurs." Sitting on numerous private and not for profit boards, he has also been an adjunct lecturer of entrepreneurship at Olin Graduate School of Business at Babson College. A nationally and internationally sought after speaker, Davis is regularly called upon by business leaders and the media as a resource on managing the challenges faced by entrepreneurial leadership and family-run organizations trying to advance and achieve greater success in today's shifting economy.

JDavis@Mageusa.com

**Mark Cohen**, Director of Human Resources at Stavis Seafoods, Inc., has vast experience as an external consultant and internal human resources leader. His diverse background includes over thirty years of working with international and US technology companies in the computer, healthcare, biotechnology, pharmaceutical, and distribution industries. Cohen's track record includes positions as Worldwide Director of Human Resources at Phillips Medical Systems and a Senior Manager at Maxtor Corporation. He also spent sixteen years in human resources management at Digital Equipment Corporation and held training and human resources positions at Fidelity, General Mills, and Polaroid.

Cohen0778@gmail.com

# AHAthat™

AHAthat makes it easy to share, author, and promote content. There are over 38,000 quotes (AHAmessages™) by thought leaders from around the world that you can share in seconds for free.

For those who want to author their own book, we have time-tested proven processes that allow you to write your AHAbook™ of 140 digestible, bite-sized morsels in eight hours or less. Once your content is on AHAthat, you have a customized link that you can use to have your fans/advocates share your content and help grow your network.

⮑ Start sharing: http://AHAthat.com

⮑ Start authoring: http://AHAthat.com/Author

Hey,
Did You
AHAthat™?

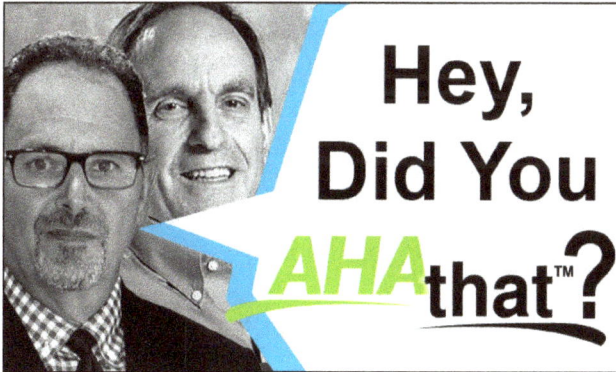

Please go directly to this book in AHAthat and share each AHAmessage socially at http://aha.pub/24turnaround.